Work Around the Clock

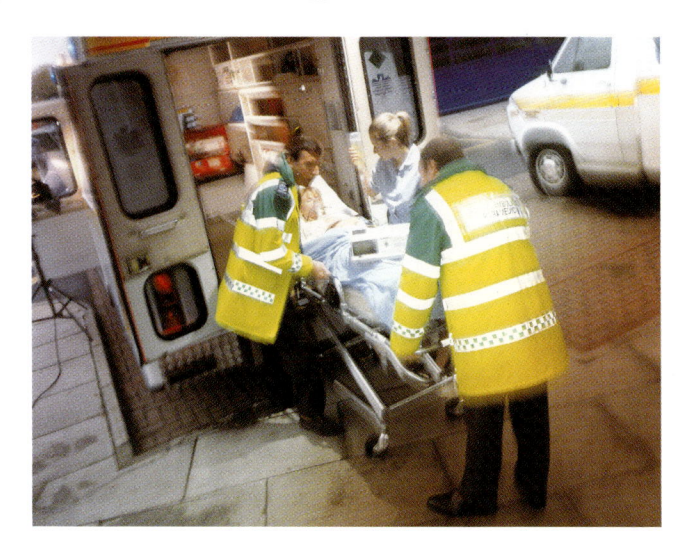

Contents

What Time Is It?	2
9:00 A.M.	3
12:00 P.M.	6
4:00 P.M.	8
7:00 P.M.	10
2:00 A.M.	12
6:00 A.M.	14
Glossary	Inside back cover
Index	Inside back cover

Michele Lyons

What Time Is It?

It's time for work! That means it's…anytime! Day or night, there's somebody, somewhere, busy at work!

9:00 A.M.

It's nine o'clock in the morning. Many jobs start at this time and last through the afternoon.

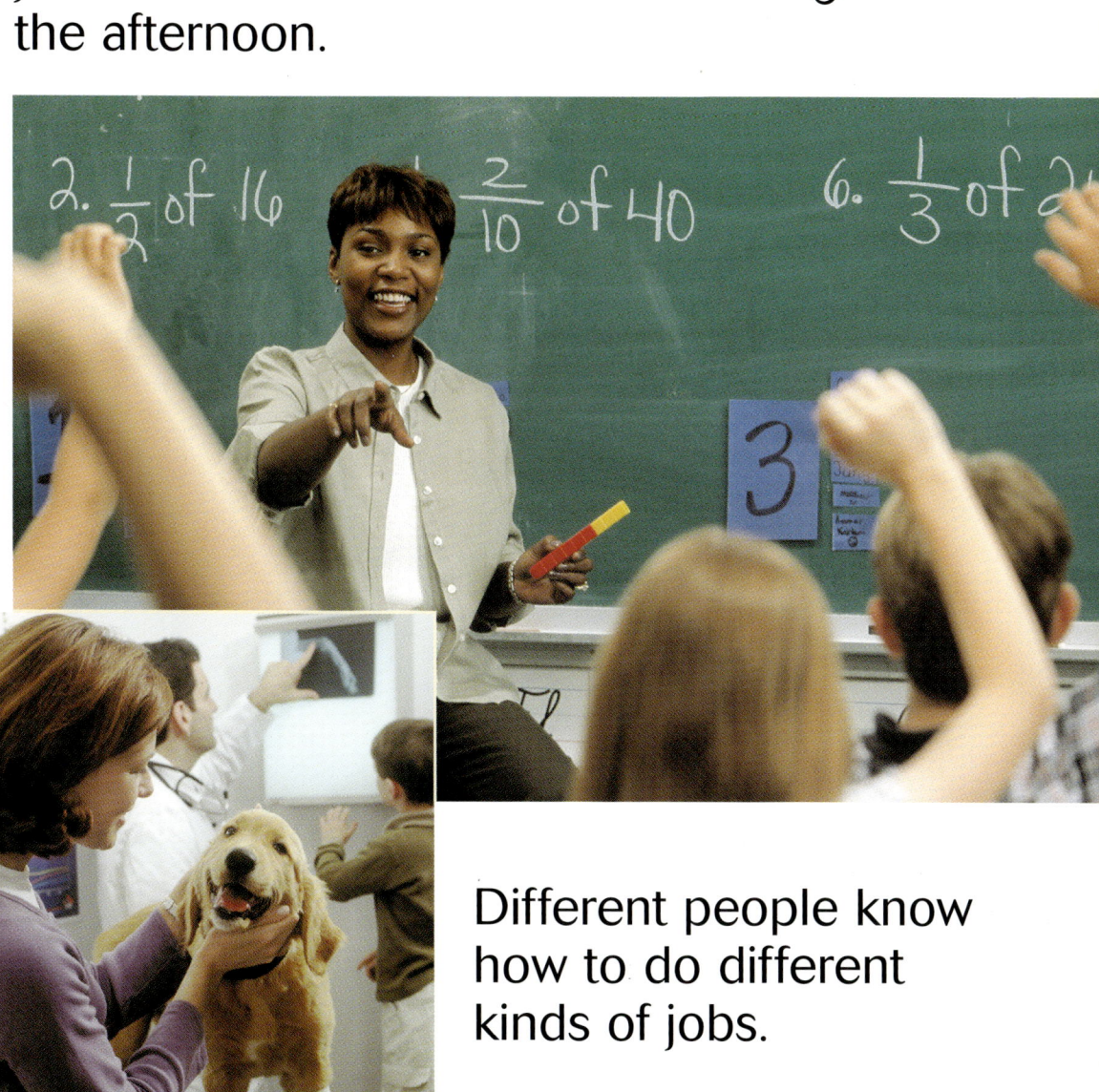

Different people know how to do different kinds of jobs.

Some workers grow or make things for people to buy. These are **goods**.

Other workers get paid for doing things for people. They provide **services**.

Most people get paid for their work. They use the money to buy things they need or want.

Sometimes people are busy working. Other times they're busy spending.

12:00 P.M.

It's noon! How do these workers help people get what they need in the middle of the day?

Cashiers are busy now. Many people use their lunch break to shop for things they need.

4:00 P.M.

Some jobs need doing all around the clock.

So some people start work in the afternoon. They work **shifts,** or take turns, so nobody gets too tired.

Bus drivers work during **rush hour** to bring people home from their jobs.

7:00 P.M.

When workers get home, they want to know what happened in the world during the day.

The **newscasters** tell them at dinnertime.

People also like to have fun in the evening. **Actors** work in the evening so people can go to plays. What other workers help people enjoy their free time?

2:00 A.M.

S-h-h-h-h! It's the middle of the night! Most people are sleeping.

But doctors and nurses are "on call" all night long in case somebody needs them.

Some people work all night to get things ready for the next day.

This worker runs a machine that prints tomorrow morning's newspaper.

6:00 A.M.

Rise and shine! Some jobs start really early in the morning. Farmers know this is a good time to start working.

Thanks to this baker, grocery stores will have fresh bagels to sell in time for breakfast.

Day or night, there's somebody, somewhere, busy at work.

When do you think these people are working?

16